GW01451605

Original title:
The Magic of Thanksgiving Moments

Author: Elias Marchant

ISBN HARDBACK: 978-9916-94-332-8
ISBN PAPERBACK: 978-9916-94-333-5

Remembrances in Roasted Roots

A turkey dressed in velvet coat,
Stands proud, though it can't gloat.
Grandpa's jokes make stomachs ache,
As Aunt Lucy burns the chocolate cake.

Pumpkin pies with crusts that flop,
We cheer as our hopes drop.
Cousin Joe's dance provokes a laugh,
While Dad's snores steal the aftermath.

Under the Autumn Sky

Leaves fall like hats, oh what a sight,
A band of squirrels begins a fight.
Gravy fountains, oh what a mess,
Mom's hairdo now in distress.

A toast with cider, bubbles fly,
Jimmy's hiccup makes us cry.
With every joke and silly trick,
We find ourselves stuck in laughter's grip.

A Day of Thanks Unfolding

Around the table, tales are spun,
Pies are blessed, and then they run.
Someone steals the last drumstick,
While Uncle Fred tells a sleepy flick.

Crackers pop and laughter rings,
Not sure what the meal really brings.
A dance-off starts with Auntie Sue,
With moves that make us all go, 'Phew!'

Hearthside Reflections

The hearth is warm, the jokes are loud,
A family feast, we're all so proud.
But who forgot the veggie tray?
Cousin Tim now starts to sway.

With hats made of napkins, we all sing,
As laughter flutters on curious wings.
A toast to mishaps and joy we share,
Together we feast, no need for despair.

Feasts of Heart and Home

Pumpkin pie battles, who can eat more?
Family debates on which chair's the score.
Uncles tell stories, but they're out of date,
Naps in the corner? That's fate, not a state.

Cranberry sauce flops, right onto the floor,
Laughter erupts, is it even a chore?
Kids run amok, like turkeys gone wild,
Grandma's got cookies, she's still such a child.

Cornucopia of Connections

A cornucopia spills, but so does the wine,
A toast turns to silliness, all is divine.
Cousins with quirks, oh, they steal the show,
Grandpa's new dance? It's a sight, oh, no!

Spuds flying high, mashed potatoes in flight,
Everyone dodges, it's quite the last sight.
With laughter and joy, we gather and share,
Even Aunt Mabel's wild hairstyle we dare.

Leaves of Thanks

Leaves tumble down in a colorful swirl,
Kids jump and shout, making it all a whirl.
Gratitude's funny, when mixed with a pie,
Mom burns the crust, and the dog starts to cry.

Thankful for foibles, we giggle and grin,
Finding old photos, where do we begin?
A toast to the flubs, and the mishaps we made,
Our hearts swell with joy, and we laugh at our trade.

Bountiful Blessings

Bountiful blessings piled high on the plate,
Relatives arguing about who's first at the gate.
Quirky traditions that make our hearts sing,
A sock puppet turkey? Oh, what will they bring!

Leftovers are treasures, a feast beyond dreams,
Whipped cream fights turn into hilarious schemes.
With laughter that echoes, we cherish the time,
These moments we savor, like a whimsical rhyme.

Family Footsteps

In the kitchen, chaos reigns,
Cousins collide like runaway trains.
A turkey's dance, a gravy splat,
Uncle Joe now wears a hat!

Kids are giggling, dogs are prancing,
Someone's pants? Oh no, they're dancing!
A family feast, where laughter roars,
And Grandma's secret rolls out the doors.

The table wobbles, the chairs all squeak,
A toddler dreams of pie to sneak.
A toast to all, with juice in hand,
Who knew this could be such a grand?

When the meal's done, the floor's a sight,
Leftover stuffing takes a flight.
With every bite, a comical tale,
Thanksgiving bliss, we can't derail!

Seasoned with Love

In the corner, spices flee,
A sprinkle here, a dash of glee.
Mom throws flour like it's confetti,
Dad's in the blender, looking quite ready.

Sweet potatoes dance on the stove,
Mashed like clouds, they proudly hove.
Brother's sneaking pie, oh what a sight,
We've got more dessert than dinner tonight!

The cranberry spills with a zesty sound,
A mishap? Hopefully, not on the ground.
As laughter mingles with buttery scents,
A cooking show? No, pure suspense!

From burnt tobs in the blink of an eye,
We taste and pretend it's all apple pie.
Yet amidst the mess and the sporadic, we find,
It's love served up, with a side of wine.

Echoes in Every Bite

Every slice tells a tale to share,
Of Aunt Lucy's green beans, a brave dare.
The pumpkin pie, a towering delight,
Is it dessert? Or just an oversight?

We chew on stories, both fresh and old,
Where laughter softens the crust of gold.
Dad's secret recipe, a twist on the norm,
In every spoonful, we weather the storm.

Friends and family gather near,
With mashed potatoes and a side of cheer.
A bite of laughter, a sprinkle of sass,
"Who's still hungry?" echoes across the mass!

The table's a battlefield, forks at the ready,
As stories flow and spirits stay heady.
In each tasty morsel, we find our delight,
Thankful and silly, we dance through the night!

A Grateful Heart's Journey

Through the front door, we tumble in,
With hugs and high fives, let the fun begin.
Savory smells lead us down the hall,
But who's that? Is it Auntie Paul?

Pies align like a sweet parade,
With whipped cream mountains that laugh and fade.
A cousin's face, stuffed with bread,
We all just grin, no words need be said.

We toast to the pets, the fridge, and the pie,
With each clink of cups, we all fly high.
Thankfulness bubbles in funny throats,
As stories retold lead to wild anecdotes.

So here's to the joy found at every seat,
In silly moments, our hearts skip a beat.
With laughter and love, we continue to sway,
On this journey of gratitude, hip-hip-hooray!

The Spirit of Abundance

Turkey on the table,
Pies stacked high, oh dear!
Granddad stole my gravy,
Now it's gone from here.

Uncle Joe keeps eating,
He claims it's all in drive.
But his belt just gave out,
And now he can't survive!

Cousins throw the rolls,
Like they're in a game,
Mom just eyes the ceiling,
She's gone fully insane.

Laughter spills like cider,
We dance like there's a chance,
In this wild dinner chaos,
Who needs a silly trance?

Celebrating Quiet Joys

The cat steals the pumpkin,
That sneaky little thief,
Every slice I try to grab,
Ends in feline grief.

Sister's got her secret,
A stash of chocolate bars,
While we munch on turkey,
She'll snack under the stars.

Grandma's recipe flops,
The stuffing's far too dry,
We choke and laugh it off,
As we all start to cry.

But amidst the giggles,
And the food that's gone awry,
We find the joy in chaos,
With a twinkle in each eye.

Candles and Conversations

Candles flicker brightly,
Casting shadows on the wall,
Auntie's rambling tales,
Make the evening crawl.

Dad's trying to impress,
With his dad jokes so old,
But we can't stop laughing,
At his puns, bold and cold.

Sister talks to her phone,
While we're here in person,
She's seeking social likes,
When our smiles should worsen.

Yet as we all gather,
Huddled tight, full of cheer,
We realize our bond,
Is what brings us all here.

Handwritten Wishes

We scribble our wishes,
On napkins of all sorts,
A dream to fly to Mars,
Or to build a giant fort.

Cousins doodle nonsense,
With crayons and bright hues,
While Auntie's secret recipe,
Is lost to her own blues.

Dad's drawing a turkey,
Looks more like a fish,
We giggle and we tease,
About his artsy wish.

Yet laughter is the gift,
That wraps around our hearts,
In this whirlwind of chaos,
Each moment truly starts.

Family Ties and Endless Skies

Gathered round the table tight,
Uncle Bob's quite a sight.
He spills the gravy, what a mess,
We laugh and sigh, but we're blessed.

Aunt Sue's secret pie is here,
With mystery filling—never clear.
Timmy's got his face in the dish,
Dreaming of cake, that's his only wish.

Cousins tussling over turkey,
Laughing loud, oh so quirky.
Dad just naps, the feast is grand,
While we plot the next prank, oh so planned.

Family ties like mashed potatoes,
Sticky bonds, bright as tomatoes.
Through all the chaos, here's the scoop,
We're the wackiest, jolly troop.

Echoes of Gratitude

Thankful hearts and goofy grins,
Whirling winds and playful spins.
Each "thanks" giggles through the air,
As fond memories start to share.

Grandma's yarn of giant turkeys,
That run away, oh those quirksies!
We laugh so hard, we start to tear,
As her tales get stranger each year.

Dad's famous joke gets thrown around,
What's the best dish? Oh, look, it's brown!
A sea of laughter, a waves of cheer,
Our echoes ring, for all to hear.

In the heart of this hilarious feast,
Our gratitude grows, not the least.
With every laugh and joyful cheer,
We count our blessings, oh so near.

Lanterns of Love on the Table

Candles flicker, food's delight,
Mom's dance moves are quite the sight.
She twirls with pie, a sight that's bold,
And shares her secrets, never told.

Sister's stuffing, a jiggly mess,
"Just one more bite!" we all confess.
Cousins cheer as we take a dare,
To try her concoction—do we care?

Uncle Jim's puns, we've heard before,
Like the jokes, we just can't ignore.
It's all in love, with laughter's grace,
As we gather 'round this happy place.

Lanterns glowing, hearts aglow,
In this warmth, our love will grow.
Tales of joy, jokes in the air,
Thankful laughter, everywhere.

Cornucopia of Memories

A table spread with food galore,
But wait! There's always room for more.
Grandpa's tales flow like the wine,
His voice so rich, it's quite divine.

The cornucopia spills out proud,
With laughter louder than the crowd.
"Oh, look! A family photo bomb!"
We giggle here, it's all part of the charm.

The dog sneaks crumbs beneath the chair,
While cousin Joe makes quite a scare.
He attempts a flip, lands on a pie,
"Oh dear!" we shout, with a joyful sigh.

Memories blend like gravy thick,
With every joke and playful trick.
In this feast of love and bliss,
It's the funny moments we won't miss.

Harvest Whispers

The turkey's dance is quite absurd,
As Aunt June trips over the bird.
Cranberry sauce flies through the air,
While cousin Bob just doesn't care.

Granddad's stories never cease,
Of his time with a raucous geese.
The pumpkin pie is looking shy,
As the dog steals it, oh my, oh my!

Laughter echoes, voices cheer,
Dad's jokes bring us all good near.
We hold our bellies with delight,
While the voices fade to night.

But the best part? It's clear and bright,
Without the dishes left in sight.
We raise our cups, a toast so grand,
To family fun that's truly planned.

Grateful Heartbeats

Upon the table, food galore,
A feathery friend we can't ignore.
Sister's mashed potatoes, what a sight,
With lumps that wiggle—quite the fright!

Uncle Joe starts his routine,
Imitating a dancing bean.
We laugh so hard, we spill our tea,
While Aunt May shouts, "Leave me be!"

Have you heard of the corn that speaks?
It told a joke and left us weak.
Pie fights break out; it's a mess!
But really, who could ever guess?

We ponder life with grins so wide,
As laughter lingers, hopes abide.
Grateful for the fun we partake,
Thankfulness is the pie we bake.

Autumn's Embrace

Leaves tumble down in a swirling spin,
As we debate whose dish should win.
Is it stuffing? Or maybe pie?
Uncle Bob claims it all is dry!

The cornucopia's full of glee,
As kids play hide and seek with the B.
A cat in the kitchen, oh what luck,
His paws all covered in yams, oh shucks!

Grandma's knitting while we feast,
Her yarn is tangled, to say the least.
We help her free the fuzzy mess,
While giggling at the family chess.

As shadows lengthen, tales unfold,
The laughter warms us from the cold.
Thankful hearts, we smile and care,
In autumn's love, we gladly share.

Feasts of Stillness

A rumbling belly breaks the calm,
Cousins munching on a breadcrumb bomb.
Turkey legs are flying wide,
While Grandma gives a watchful guide.

Whispers of pie are in the air,
Mom's secret recipe to share!
But oh dear Bob, he's lost his plate,
Now searching beneath the great crate!

The table's set with leaves and cheer,
But spills bring laughter, never fear.
We navigate with forks held high,
Discussing who will dance and why.

At dusk we gather, spirits bright,
With full bellies and hearts alight.
In stillness, joy takes its stance,
As we share a bountiful glance.

Pinecone and Pumpkin

A pinecone sat on the table,
Wearing a hat, feeling quite stable.
The pumpkins rolled in with a grin,
Saying, "We're all just waiting to win!"

The corn had a dance, it was silly,
Popping around, oh what a thrill-y!
While potatoes mashed with a clatter,
Claiming they were the main dish batter!"

The turkey waddled, puffed out his chest,
Said, "I'm the guest of honor, at best!"
The pinecone chuckled with glee,
"Let's have some fun, just you and me!"

As laughter filled the cozy hall,
The dishes said, "We're here for the brawl!"
With laughter and joy shared 'round our feast,
Even the veggies had joined the beast!

The Art of Giving Thanks

A gourd dressed up in a bow tie,
Said, "Why not ask me why I fly?"
Carrots chimed in, "We're roots of fun!"
"We'll help you celebrate, one by one!"

The gravy boat wobbled, a funny thing,
"I flow like rivers, come watch me swing!"
Stuffing rolled in, a fluffy surprise,
"Together we'll sparkle, watch us rise!"

The table was set, what a display,
Even the napkins danced in a sway.
With laughter and love, we raised a glass,
Who would've thought? A meal could amass!"

So here's to the chuckles and tasty bites,
To moments of joy that ignite our nights.
Let's toss our worries, let laughter trade,
For this is the art we've gleefully made!

A Symphony of Flavors

In a pot, the spices had a ball,
Chili and garlic both answered the call.
"Add a dash of humor," said salt with a cheer,
"It spices up life, let's make it clear!"

Sage played the flute, while thyme joined in,
The onions sang songs, their notes were a win.
The garlic danced wildly, twirling around,
While the pepper cracked jokes that made laughter
abound!

The casserole joined with a crunchy delight,
Each layer a story, each bite outta sight.
A symphony savory and sweet on the plate,
As we gobbled it up, it was purely first-rate!

So raise your forks high, let out a cheer,
For this feast we've made is the highlight of the year.
With laughter and flavor, our hearts intertwine,
In this orchestra of tastes, everything's fine!

From Our Family to Yours

Gather 'round, folks, it's time to eat,
We've cooked up a storm, it's quite the feat!
A pie that's wobbly, not quite sincere,
Looks like it's dancing from ear to ear!

The kids are in charge of the coconut cake,
Launching sprinkles like confetti with each quick shake.
Mom's in the corner, just shaking her head,
"We've gagged on dessert? Where's the bread?"

With crazy hats made of leftover rolls,
Grandpa's the star, he's stealing the bowls.
From laughing too hard at a joke gone wrong,
To finding the turkey, we all chant along.

So here's to the moments we'll cherish and keep,
With laughter and love, and memories deep.
From our family to yours, we send a toast,
To the joy of good food—oh we love it the most!

Leaves of Gratitude

The turkey wobbles, what a sight,
Grandma's dance, so out of sight.
Cousin Joe trips on a chair,
A feast so grand, who'd ever care?

Pumpkin pie falls with a splat,
Uncle Bob yells, 'Where's the cat?'
Family laughter fills the air,
Thankful hearts, a little flair!

A dog sneaks food right off the plate,
While Grandpa snores, oh isn't that great?
Gravy spills on Auntie Sue,
But who cares, we all want two!

With every wink and every cheer,
We gobble up the joy right here.
Mismatched socks are quite the trend,
Thankful love we all extend!

Whispers of Autumn's Feast

The table's set, a crooked line,
Where Aunt May claims her pie's divine.
Cousins bicker over stuffing,
While everyone's eyes are a bit puffing.

Floating scents of sweet delight,
A missed catch leads to a food fight.
With cranberry juice on the wall,
It's a feast, let laughter call!

Apple cider overflows the cup,
While the turkey waves, 'What's up?'
Dad's secret recipe goes awry,
'It's burnt, but hey, let's just try!'

With funny hats and silly games,
Every dish has its own claims.
In this chaos, love's the prize,
As laughter dances in our eyes!

Nurtured in Tradition

Granddad's stories have no end,
Each verse bent around the bend.
He guffaws, we nod and sip,
As pie slips off his mighty grip.

The kids race round, a blur of fun,
While Grandma counts, 'Oh, just one.'
The turkey's timer rings away,
But who can hear amidst the play?

Cousin Sally's hat, too tall,
Towers over us all, a wall!
She tries to dance, her moves so wild,
We laugh as if we are all a child.

From silly jokes to pumpkin seeds,
These quirky moments are our needs.
Wrapped in warmth of laughter's glow,
With grateful hearts, we let love flow!

Stories Shared Over Pie

Two forks battle for the last slice,
The cat pounces, 'Oh, not so nice!'
Chairs creak as tales unfold,
Each one funnier than the old.

The pie takes center stage tonight,
With whipped cream clouds, a dreamy sight.
Auntie's secret? 'It's all a sham!'
While the cat snatches bits from ham.

Laughter rings like church bells sound,
As we gather round, joy unbound.
A toast with soda, clever and spry,
'Here's to every laugh and pie!'

Through ups and downs, we find our way,
In this joyful, silly play.
These moments shared, sweet as the pie,
Forever cherished, oh my, oh my!

Candles, Cornbread, and Kindness

Candles flicker, shadows play,
Cornbread crumbles, what a day!
Uncle Joe's jokes, they fly like kites,
As Grandma scolds him for food fights.

Plates stacked high with all the treats,
A turkey dance that can't be beat!
Cousins giggle, mom rolls her eyes,
In this craziness, joy surely lies.

A heartfelt toast begins to rise,
Pies are cooling, oh what a prize!
Laughter echoes, spills from the room,
We're all grateful for chaos and gloom.

So bring on the food and the hearty cheer,
These wacky moments, we hold so dear!
Candles might melt, and cornbread might fall,
But kindness will wrap us, here one and all.

A Tapestry of Togetherness

Thankful threads in colors bright,
Gather 'round, it's quite a sight!
Aunt Sally's knitting, tangled and wild,
Even the cat joined in, that naughty child.

Socks for gifts, we all did groan,
But the fruitcake was worse, it could moan!
Grandpa's pie with a side of sass,
One tiny slice? We'll break the glass.

The table's set, but wait—oh no!
Someone's spilled the gravy flow!
Old tales rise, like turkey steam,
Together, we share the silliest dream.

In this tapestry of quirks and cheer,
Love and laughter pull us near.
Through mishaps and blunders, it's all understood,
Together, we weave our own kind of good.

Remnants of Joy

Leftover turkey, a dog's delight,
Even the fridge is a funny sight.
Cranberry sauce, a sticky foe,
Wrestle it out? Oh, give it a throw!

Mismatched socks, still on the floor,
Last night's chatter, who could ignore?
Grandma's old chair creaks with pride,
Whispers of laughter, side by side.

With bits of joy, we made a feast,
Count the blessings, at least one beast.
A stray veggie dance, a salad too,
All remnants of love we keep anew.

In corners of hearts, smiling wide,
These goofy moments, we won't hide.
With joyful remnants, oh what a mess,
We gather the laughter, nothing less!

The Comfort of Old Recipes

Old recipes whisper from dusty books,
Grandma's secrets, and quirky looks.
Mixing and stirring, oh what a thrill,
A pinch of delight, just add some sill!

From burnt to golden, the journey's a jest,
Each dish tells stories, who likes them best?
Fudge gone wrong and cookies that flop,
With laughter in kitchens, we just can't stop.

The recipe calls for a cup of cheer,
Add a dash of chaos, lend me your ear!
Split the pie with grandma's grin,
These timeless dishes, where do we begin?

As we gather 'round and happily dine,
Savor the flavors, both yours and mine.
With old recipes and newer pranks,
We feast in joy, oh, who needs thanks?

Embracing Moments of Stillness

In a kitchen chaos, pots do clang,
But Aunt Sue's dance moves make us all sang.
A turkey that wobbles, a pie that's askew,
Laughter erupts as the mishaps ensue.

Uncle Joe spills gravy on Grandma's new dress,
She gives him a glare, then reverts to her jest.
"Who needs a runway? Just call me a star!"
He twirls and he trips—it's a laugh from afar.

A table set neatly, then comes Cousin Pete,
He drops his whole plate—oh, what a defeat!
Yet everyone chuckles, with joy in the air,
Mom says, "Don't worry, there's plenty to share!"

As moments pass by, we sit and we smile,
In the midst of the chaos, stay for a while.
For messy and funny, they blend with the cheer,
In one lovely gathering, our hearts draw near.

Harvest Moonlight

Under a sky with stars shining bright,
We roast marshmallows, a delightful sight.
Uncle Bob tells tales, some quite far-fetched,
As the kids all giggle, their eyebrows are stretched.

A pumpkin that wobbles, a game of catch,
Cousins run wild, it's quite the mismatch.
"Who threw that squash?" "Not me!" is the cry,
Our laughter erupts as it soars through the sky.

A dog named Rufus steals chips from the spread,
Chasing him down, we all end up red.
While Grandma just shakes her head in despair,
"Just don't let him eat all the food, I swear!"

With laughter and stories, the evening unfolds,
As heartwarming moments become tales that are told.
In this late-night glow, with moonlight so clear,
Family together, it's best time of year!

The Warmth of Familiar Faces

Gathered together, those faces we know,
Sister's high-pitched laugh is the grandest show.
Dad's jokes land flat, but we love him the same,
Especially when he forgets grandma's name!

Aunt Lucy brings cookies, they vanish too fast,
"Are those really cookies or just dust from the past?"
We feast on the memories, we cherish them well,
And Uncle Fred always seems to give a good yell.

Fighting over who gets the last bit of pie,
"Hey, hands off my slice!"—oh, my oh my!
But in all the bickering, love fills the room,
With warm, silly moments, we endlessly bloom.

As we gather around, with candles aglow,
The warmth of our faces, the love we all show.
In this jolly chaos, we find what we seek,
The glue of our hearts grows stronger each week.

Nature's Palette

Leaves rustle softly, a colorful swirl,
Dad trips on a branch, oh how we all twirl!
Balloons in the air, a mishap that's sweet,
Each pop sends us laughing, oh what a treat!

Nature provides colors, red, gold, and green,
While Cousin Sam dreams of a life on the screen.
"I'll catch that big turkey!" he proudly proclaims,
But ends up in leaves, mixing up all the names.

Pumpkin spice lattes spill over the side,
A comedy act as we all try to hide.
With sips and with spills, there's fun on the run,
In moments like these, we share warmth like the sun.

So here's to the blunders, the laughter we find,
Every messy moment, joy intertwined.
In the palette of people, laughter's our art,
With each funny flub, we grow closer at heart.

Dreams Served Warm

Turkey's dancing on the table,
Pumpkin pie begins to fable.
Cousin Brad plays air guitar,
Grandma's cooking, it's bizarre.

Cranberries bounce like rubber balls,
Uncle Joe slips and nearly falls.
Laughter fills the cozy room,
Even Aunt Sue joined the zoom!

Kids are sneaking snacks galore,
While the dog is eyeing more.
With every hug and silly grin,
Thanksgiving fun's about to begin.

So toast to joys and all we share,
With awkward stories everywhere!
We feast and play, it's quite the show,
Memories made as we overflow.

Love in Every Bite

The turkey trips across the floor,
While grandma yells, "That's not for sure!"
Aunties gossip in the musty air,
While Grandpa snokes about 'that hair.'

Potatoes whipped with flair and might,
Moms compare whose dish is right.
We nibble, chomp, and slurp with glee,
While Dad attempts a dance, oh, me!

The casserole dishes form a wall,
As second servings start to call.
In every bite, there's love to find,
With laughs that linger, oh so kind.

And when we think we've had enough,
There's pie, and yes, that's the tough stuff.
With faces sticky, hearts so light,
This feast is pure and yet, a delight.

Thanksgiving Tides

Gather 'round, it's nearly time,
To gobble gobs of food sublime.
The table shakes with every cheer,
As Uncle Lou cracks jokes, oh dear!

Cranberry sauce in wobble form,
A family buffet, that's the norm.
Kids take bets on who will trip,
And can Aunt May really cook or sip?

The dog has got a master plan,
To snatch a leg bone from the man.
While laughter rolls like tasty tides,
Our goofy crew, the joy abides.

So raise a glass with silly grins,
To all the chaos where fun begins.
With every dish we have this night,
Thanksgiving brings pure delight.

A Melody of Memories

A clatter here, a clink and clank,
As brother's pulled a turkey prank.
Mom's face is priceless, oh so bright,
As laughter takes its joyful flight.

Each casserole has a funny name,
Like 'Aunt June's dish of shame.'
We poke and laugh, we snatch a bite,
As stories make the evening light.

Grandpa, with his tales so tall,
While sibling rivalries enthrall.
We play a game with goofy rules,
As chaos reigns and laughter fuels.

With every hug and story shared,
Our hearts grow full, and none are spared.
So here's to laughter and delight,
In this melody, we take flight.

Heartstrings and Tablecloths

Around the table, we all collide,
Gravy rivers, mashed potato tides.
Uncle Joe spills wine, what a sight!
A toast to chaos, cheers with delight.

A pie that fell, oh what a show,
Grandma eye rolls, her hands on her toe.
Cousin Tim's dance, a turkey tango,
We laugh till we snort, oh how we glow.

Stuffing battles, who can hold more?
Sibling rivalry, who's keeping score?
A turkey leg toss, a clumsy dad,
Thankful for moments, a bit goofy, but glad.

When bellies ache and laughter flows,
Family ties, everyone knows.
With heartstrings woven, the day unfolds,
In silly moments, our love is bold.

Echoes of Laughter

At the door, the laughter spills,
Jokes and jests with buttered pills.
A knock-knock joke, Dad can't take,
As Aunt May grins, ``Make no mistake!``

The dog steals turkey, oh what a thief,
As everyone gasps, disbelief!
We chase him down, what a wild game,
Caught him munching, we can't blame.

Grandma's recipe, she shares with flair,
A pinch of this and a dash of care.
But when she sneezes, spices take flight,
The whole room erupts, what a sight!

Around the table, we hold our plates,
As laughter echoes, no room for fates.
In every bite, there's joy to taste,
In of our hearts, these moments won't waste.

Gathering Under Golden Skies

Underneath the bright blue dome,
We gather here, far from home.
Kids racing like wild turkeys loose,
Whispers of pie, with sauce to juice.

The sun sets low, a glorious fire,
Roasting marshmallows, one true desire.
A cousin slips, falls in the grass,
Grinning a wide oyster smile, what a class!

A game of charades, goofy poses,
Each act more ridiculous, no one dozes.
A hat made of leaves, oh the fashion fright,
We laugh so hard, hearts feeling light.

As stars twinkle like mischief in eyes,
We share our tales and silly tries.
With every hug, the bond renews,
In these moments, we can't lose.

Recipes of Affection

In the kitchen, a dash of cheer,
A sprinkle of laughter, merry and clear.
Mom's secret recipe, oh what a treat,
But it's mostly just cookies we hope to eat!

Sisters in aprons, flour in the air,
The dog's on a mission, with hopes to share.
Pies on the counter, right on the brink,
He's snatched a slice, oh, what do you think?

Dad's behind the grill, flipping with flair,
Burnt offerings found, nothing to spare!
Giggles erupt at the charred black meat,
But with a glass of cheer, it's still a feat!

With every dish, there's laughter infused,
Memories made, and all feeling amused.
It's not just food, but love that we serve,
In this gathering, we waltz and swerve.

From Fields to Feast

In a field of corn, we took a stroll,
Found a turkey playing baseball, on a roll.
He swung a bat, with all his might,
We laughed so hard, what a silly sight.

Granny's pie had a mind of its own,
It wobbled and jiggled, like a happy grown.
The dog tried to catch it on a spree,
But pie won the race, running wild and free.

Mashed potatoes joined a conga line,
They twirled and twisted, feeling so fine.
A disco ball made of salad greens,
Shimmered and shook in our joyful scenes.

Dinner bells rang, the turkey got wise,
He donned a hat, much to our surprise.
"Not today folks!" he clucked with cheer,
"I'm off to be a star, so grab some beer!"

Whims of the Season

The leaves were dancing, swirling around,
As squirrels collected nuts, acting quite profound.
One tried a cartwheel, fell flat on his face,
We couldn't stop laughing, what a clumsy race.

At the table sat Uncle Joe all spry,
He wore a pumpkin hat, oh my oh my!
With mashed potato mustache, he looked quite grand,
We cheered him on, a true one-man band.

Cousin Susie brought her singing supply,
A turkey costume that made us all cry.
She belted out tunes, the turkey joined in,
A feast of laughter, let the good times begin!

Mom served the pie, but oh what a shock,
The whipped cream squirted, just like a clock.
With laughter echoing, a blob on the floor,
We gasped and giggled, "Can we have more?"

The Kindness in Our Hearts

A little old lady with a heart of gold,
Took her cat to dinner, or so I've been told.
Mr. Whiskers wore a festive bow tie,
As he reached for turkey, we all heard a sigh.

The pumpkins gathered, forming a choir,
Singing off-key, with all of their fire.
They puffed out their cheeks, and made quite a sound,
Wishing us all joy, as laughter abound.

Cousin Billy tried to juggle some bread,
But dropped the rolls, crashed hard on his head.
With a wink and a grin, he said, "Hey, it's fine,
At least I can eat, while I sip my wine!"

With loving heart, we shared a grand toast,
To family, laughter, and what means the most.
For in the chaos, love truly shines,
Through giggles and warmth, across all our lines.

Notes of Nostalgia

A photo appeared of grandpa so spry,
In a turkey suit, oh me, oh my!
He danced on the table, you couldn't believe,
The food took a moment, just to reprieve.

A toast went awry, with splashes and cheers,
Soaked Uncle Frank, in giggles and jeers.
With laughter like gravy, he wiped off his specs,
And claimed it was part of his holiday flex.

Old stories were shared, of flops and of fumbles,
A pie on the ceiling, had us all in jumbles.
We laughed until we cried, our hearts feeling light,
In that sweet, silly moment, everything felt right.

So here's to the past, with a wink and a nod,
For the laughter and joy, we're ever so awed.
Thanksgiving this year, may it always bring cheer,
With funny old memories, we hold oh so dear.

Unity in Every Slice

Gather 'round the table wide,
Where turkey and mashed potatoes collide.
Uncle Bob tells jokes with glee,
While Aunt Sue spills her iced tea.

Every slice brings laughter near,
As we toast with soda and cheer.
Mystery casseroles do appear,
Taste tests spark a little fear!

Carving skills put to the test,
Who knew we'd all be so blessed?
With every bite, a story is spun,
And Grandpa's snore is just too fun!

In the end, we all agree,
This meal's a mixed melody.
From knotted napkins to spilled pies,
Thankful for all the quirky ties!

Gratitude in Full Bloom

Flowers on the table thrive,
While Cousin Jake plays the live jive.
We dance with gravy, slip on peas,
As laughter floats upon the breeze.

Pumpkin pie with an absurd hat,
A sweet turkey that looks like a cat.
With each delicious, quirky bite,
We toast to friends who bring delight.

Thankful for what's fresh and new,
Even if Aunt Patty's stew,
Tastes more like a science fair,
We say we like it—what a dare!

Around the harvest, stories flow,
And silly moments steal the show.
With every giggle and every tune,
We feast like wolves beneath the moon.

Reflections on a Rustic Table

Rustic wood, a family feast,
Where every dish could be a beast!
Mashed potatoes with weird shapes,
As we all critique the drapes.

Reflections bounce in shiny plates,
A family photo? Uh-oh, debates!
Grandma's sweater, quite a fright,
But her turkey? Pure delight!

Candles flicker with a hop,
Grandpa's tale? Please, make it stop!
Yet under smiles, we share the bliss,
A simple family moment, we won't miss.

Through turkey crumbs and laughter loud,
We're thankful for this raucous crowd.
With every slice and every cheer,
We feel alive, together here!

Traditions Woven in Time

Every year, the same old game,
We blame the turkey for being lame.
A race to the dessert table here,
Where pie fights bring us holiday cheer!

A toast to memories baked and made,
With jiggly desserts no one's afraid.
From silly hats to quirky feats,
We share our love with special eats.

Napkin fights and playful shoves,
As we're reminded just how much we love.
Traditions change, but hearts stay true,
Finding joy, just me and you.

In laughter echoing through the years,
We celebrate joy mix'd with tears.
With every hug and every rhyme,
We find our magic, we weave our time!

Serendipity in Sweet Potatoes

In the kitchen, chaos reigns,
An orange mess, with sweet terrains.
A dance of peas, they slip and slide,
While Uncle Joe takes a wild ride.

The turkey's lost, the gravy's stout,
Who knows what this fuss is about?
Mashed potatoes fly like rockets,
A feast of fun, who needs the brackets?

Pumpkin pies with wobbly crusts,
We laugh so hard, in laughter we trust.
A veggie thief snags a green bean,
And all of us burst at the scene.

In a whirl of joy, we share our snacks,
In the chaos, nobody lacks.
With smiles aplenty on this delightful day,
Serendipity rules, come what may.

Harvest Moonlit Conversations

Beneath the moon, we gather near,
Sharing tales, we all hold dear.
A squirrel mocks from a nearby tree,
While Grandpa snorts with glee, oh me!

Cornstalks sway to the banter's tune,
"Did you hear that?" a voice like a loon.
With pumpkin spice in every cup,
We giggle as the clumsy sister trips up.

The warm scent of cider fills the air,
As friends spill secrets, laughter everywhere.
"A turkey talker!" they all exclaim,
And soon the turkey's part of the game!

Under stars, our stories blend,
In moonlit joy, the night won't end.
With whims and giggles, we toast to the fun,
Harvesting memories, one by one.

Whirlwinds of Warmth

A whirlwind twirls through my grandma's kitchen,
Where butter and laughter meet with a mission.
In every corner, a scent so divine,
While cousins plot pranks with glimmers that shine.

"Pass the rolls!" someone shouts with glee,
But they fly like frisbees, oh dear me!
A whoopee cushion hides under a chair,
And Auntie's giggles fill the air.

Candied yams dance like spunky kids,
While secret recipes stay well hid.
"More pumpkin pie!" the chorus sings loud,
As everyone tries to swaddle the crowd.

With full bellies and spirits so high,
The days of our lives are like a pie.
In a whirlwind of warmth, family we cherish,
In moments of joy, no one would perish.

Leaves of Gold and Stories Untold

Amidst the leaves, we gather and play,
With laughter and stories that light up the day.
A pile so high, we jump with glee,
But watch out for that sneaky bee!

In grandma's arms, tales spin and twirl,
With ghostly grins that make us whirl.
"Remember when?" the echoes ensue,
Like popcorn popping, they pop out of the blue.

As pies cool off on window sills,
The air is sweet with the homey frills.
Lost in tales of old and bold,
We dance in wonder, our hearts to uphold.

With leaves of gold and stories swirl,
We embrace these moments, let joy unfurl.
With laughter that links us, a merry parade,
In delightful chaos, our memories are made.

Rustic Gatherings

In a quaint little cabin, we all squeeze in,
Pumpkin spice lattes, let the fun begin.
Grandpa tells stories, a turkey's great flight,
While the cat's on the table, ready to bite.

A mishap with gravy, it flies through the air,
A splash on Aunt Betty, but she doesn't care.
We'll laugh until our stomachs are sore,
As Dad wears a napkin like a crazy decor.

The kids chase each other, with pie on their face,
Uncle Joe's dancing, oh what a disgrace!
We dodge flying turkeys, we duck and we weave,
In this rustic gathering, we truly believe.

As night settles in, the stars start to glow,
We sip on our cider, feeling the flow.
With friends and with family, our hearts feel so warm,
In this delightful chaos, we weather each storm.

Thankful Hearts and Hands

Around the big table, hands piled in heaps,
We hold onto stories, and memories we keep.
A toast to the year that brought us so luck,
And to Uncle Fred's attempt to roast a big duck.

The pie starts to wobble, we all begin to stare,
Then Grandma exclaims there's too much to share!
With love we dive in, a feast of delight,
And we giggle at Cousin Tim, who's lost in a fright.

With smiles all around, and a few silly jokes,
We're thankful for laughter and all of our folks.
As plates start to empty, we stumble and sigh,
Then someone shouts, "Hey, who pieced out the pie?"

In this merry gathering, with hearts open wide,
We cherish these moments, our hearts swell with pride.
With thankful hands raised, let's give a big cheer,
For nothing's more special than family right here.

Embracing Each Bite

With forks in the air, we eagerly dive,
Into roasts and potatoes, oh, what a vibe!
Gravy and stuffing, a comfort to savor,
But who keeps on stealing my sweet potato flavor?

A sprinkle of chaos, as someone yells "Stop!"
While Aunt May's zucchini takes a floppy plop.
Each bite is a mystery, with flavors galore,
As we try not to fight over who gets more.

The laughter grows louder, as dessert rolls on in,
A mound of whipped cream, I just must begin.
The pies start to wiggle, and with just one last bite,
Our laughter erupts like the best kind of flight.

With a belly so full, and a grin ear to ear,
We dodged all the calories, but kept up good cheer.
In this feast of pure joy, we savor and smile,
Embracing each bite, let's linger a while.

Conversation Amidst the Harvest

The table is set, and oh what a sight,
Chatting and chuckling, all feels just right.
Aunt April spills cider, but we're none too shy,
As Grandpa insists he can still juggle pie.

Conversations flow like gravy on mash,
With tales full of laughter, our hearts made of cash.
"Remember the time you burnt down the roast?"
We repeat the old stories, celebrating the most.

Amidst every bite, a new joke comes unfurled,
From gaffes of the past, to blunders we're hurled.
The laughter rises higher, like leaves in the breeze,
Together we share these sweet moments with ease.

As night drapes us softly, all snug and bright,
We whisper our dreams, as the stars take their flight.
In conversations like these, with laughter our guide,
We find joy in togetherness, warmth multiplied.

Unity in Conversations

In the kitchen, pots are clanging,
Grandma's stories are still hanging.
Uncle Joe's jokes, a bit off-key,
But laughter echoes wild and free.

Sister sneezes, turkey's flying,
Cousins giggle, no denying.
Mom's face turns a shade of red,
As the dog sneaks off with bread.

The Spirit of Togetherness

Tables set, the pie arrives,
But that's when Aunt Sue's luck dives.
'Is this enough?' she asks with glee,
As others whisper, 'Just wait and see.'

Napkins tossed like paper planes,
Cousin Bob spills gravy remains.
With every bite, we share a smile,
And laugh about it all the while.

Treasures from the Table

Mashed potatoes mountain high,
But who forgot to bake the pie?
Sister says it's all just perfect,
Yet Dad can't help but interject.

While turkey reigns, desserts unite,
Pie fights spark a tasty delight.
The feast becomes a playful game,
As plates spin wild, oh what a fame!

Remnants of the Past

Each year the tales start rolling in,
About the bird that almost swam.
Aunt Mary swears it wasn't her,
While we stave off another stir.

Memories wrapped in tasty bites,
Fuzzy socks for comfy nights.
We share our joys, our playful gripes,
In the chaos, love truly types.

Heartfelt Bonds in Every Bite

Gather 'round the turkey, my old pal,
Uncle Joe's carving looks like a howler,
Grandma's pie is worth a long debate,
We'll take a chance and hope it won't grate.

Cousins throwing rolls, what a wild sight,
A game of dodge with bread, oh so bright,
Laughter erupts with each silly throw,
Guess who's cleaning up? Oh, what a show!

Aunt Sue spills gravy right on her shoe,
We all just snicker, it's what we do,
Pass the request for more whipped cream,
Just don't ask me, it's not my dream!

But through all the chaos, hugs are exchanged,
In each silly mishap, love is arranged,
A toast to our quirks, a feast from the heart,
In each wobbly moment, we never drift apart.

Abundance in Simple Moments

Sit down, feast up, there's plenty to share,
Who wants the leg? Stand back if you dare!
Mashed potatoes piled like a snowy hill,
As long as it's gravy, I'll eat my fill.

Collard greens joined by some fruitcake's plight,
Who said that fruitcake's not tasty and bright?
Mom's hidden stuffing causes quite a fuss,
Will we find it again? Well, that's a plus!

Knives clash with forks, a comical dance,
Each bite's accompanied by laughter and chance,
Dessert's a showdown, no room for restraint,
Just don't tell my waistline, it's all so quaint!

But amidst full plates and louder cheers,
This gathering warms hearts, banishes fears,
No matter the chaos, the love will stay,
In these simple moments, we find our way.

Remembrance on Each Plate

A hint of nostalgia fills up the room,
Like Aunt Beth's casserole, it fights off gloom,
Forgotten recipes that come back alive,
Like Grandma's stories, where all tales thrive.

Every dish a memory, a quirky delight,
Dad's special rules on how to hold tight,
To a piece of turkey or jam that's too sweet,
We laugh until we fall off our seat!

Tip the cranberry can with a loud squish,
"Close your eyes and wish," oh, that's the dish!
We capture these moments, a colorful plate,
In each little bite, it's love that's our fate.

So here's to the flavors that tickle our minds,
Remembrance served with silly designs,
With every chuckle and every embrace,
Thankfulness shines - oh, what a place!

Time Woven with Savor

The clock may tick, but we lose track,
When Mom serves soup, not letting us slack,
We pass the potatoes, a buttery dance,
Careful not to spill, or take a chance!

With each turkey sandwich, we share a grin,
The secret ingredient? A little sin!
Dad's old stories get taller each year,
Mixing laughter in every bite, oh dear!

Desserts descend like a sugary storm,
Where calories don't count, that's the norm,
Be careful, my friends, as pies start to fly,
After a full plate, who's brave to try?

Yet in moments so messy, that's where we shine,
In every misstep, our hearts intertwine,
Time weaves our stories as flavors collide,
In laughter, in feast, forever we ride.

Fireside Tales of Thanks

Around the fire, we gather 'round,
With tales of turkeys that fell to the ground.
Grandpa's sock, the one that he wore,
Got lost in a cheer, oh what a score!

The dog stole a roll, it was quite a scene,
While Auntie Lou asked, 'Do we have more green?'
With laughter and cider, we toast yet again,
To friends, family, and our dear little pets!

The pumpkin pie trembles, it's ready to flee,
As Uncle Joe tries to dance with a bee.
A toast to mishaps, and moments so bright,
Thanksgiving's a show, a true delight!

So let's raise our glasses and sing with delight,
For all of the blunders that went on last night.
With smiles and laughter, we'll gather once more,
At the fireside, sharing tales we adore.

A Symphony of Culinary Colors

A green bean casserole, oh what a sight,
Count the marshmallows, oh, do it right!
Mashed potatoes gleaming with butter so gold,
Uncle Bob's secret: it never gets old!

The turkey is dancing, or was that my niece?
With cranberry juice, we make quite the feast.
Pumpkin spice latte, in a really bad mug,
Two sips in, and we're all ready to hug!

Sweet potatoes twinkle with brown sugar flair,
Like the dress Aunt Joan wears, we just can't compare.
Fedora on Grandpa, and pie on his chin,
The colors of fall make our hearts quickly spin!

So let's sing a song with a fork in our hand,
Dinner time's magic, just perfectly planned.
With giggles and jokes, we'll savor each bite,
In this smorgasbord world, everything feels right!

Cherished Plates and Endless Laughter

Plates piled high with treasures galore,
Mom's stuffing is famous, it's hard to ignore.
But what is that smell? Oh no, not the pie!
Dad's gone and burnt it—oh my, oh my!

Around the table, wild stories will fling,
Of Aunt May's long mustache, and how her cat sings.
We pass the veggies and laugh 'til we weep,
While Uncle Larry snores in a mashed-potato heap!

The dog with the turkey leg eyes that shine,
Oh, go on! Just give him a nibble of brine.
With hugs and high-fives, we feast and we cheer,
Mom's calling us back; it's dessert time, my dear!

So here's to the moments that sparkle and glow,
With cherished plates filled to the brim as we go.
In laughter and love, we find our true sense,
Thankfulness wraps us, it's utterly dense!

Blessings Wrapped in Autumn Hues

In autumn's embrace, we gather with joy,
Grandma's knitted sweater, much too big for the boy.
Potatoes in bow ties, a sight to behold,
While stories from childhood are bravely retold.

A cornucopia spills out jokes and delight,
While someone miscounts and we feign a fright.
With glasses raised high, may our troubles be small,
And joy wrap around us, like leaves in the fall!

Cider spills out like stories from lips,
As we share secrets—oh, those little quips!
Turkeys and gluten-free pies on the side,
With blessings all around, there's nowhere to hide.

So as we dig in and savor what's grand,
With laughter and love, we all take a stand.
For every odd moment, we'll give thanks anew,
Wrapped in smiles and warmth, there's always more crew!

Overflowing Bowls of Memory

Grandma's soup is bubbling hot,
A meal for kings, or just a lot.
Cousins sneak a cheeky taste,
With spoons and laughter, no time to waste.

A turkey dance, all done with flair,
Uncles spinning in the air.
Pumpkin pies and whipped cream fights,
Who knew food could spark such delights?

A chair with wheels, and off he goes,
Rolling past the feast like a pro.
Dodge the green bean with a grin,
Quickest eater sure to win!

So here we gather, loud and bright,
Silly stories in the night.
With every bite, a giggle flows,
In bowls of memories, love just grows.

Stars in the Autumn Sky

The leaves all fall in jolly piles,
Kids dive in, all with big smiles.
Mom's in the kitchen baking bread,
While Dad's outside with a turkey head.

Under the stars, the firelight gleams,
S'mores made by the craziest teams.
The marshmallows dance as we eat,
Add in some joy, make it a treat!

A cat steals a roll, sneaky and sly,
Not for the feast, but to watch us cry.
Laughter erupts as we chase the cat,
Thanksgiving chaos, oh imagine that!

We count our blessings, and then we scheme,
To stuff our faces, that's the dream.
Under the stars, with hearts so spry,
Thankful for laughter beneath the sky.

A Celebration of Gratitude

Around the table, stories unfold,
With little ones dreamt in the cold.
Dad slips the turkey a sly little wink,
While Auntie's eyes twinkle, maybe she'll drink.

The wine flows freely, spills too, oh dear!
"More gravy!" cries someone, "Bring it near!"
Potatoes piled like fluffy clouds,
Our laughter booming, growing loud in crowds.

Each cousin competes for the biggest bite,
While the dog sneaks treats when out of sight.
We toast to the year, to the fun we share,
And giggles bubble up, floating through the air.

So here's to the memories, both wild and sweet,
Thankful for each goofy feat.
In every clink of glass, we find a way,
To celebrate life, come what may!

Toasting to Togetherness

With napkins tucked in and hats awry,
A toast begins, oh my oh my!
Silly shenanigans take the stage,
With granddad's jokes that never age.

Mashed potatoes fly like fluffy bombs,
More laughter erupts than digital psalms.
Aunt makes a pie, but it's burnt to black,
Still, in our hearts, it's a tasty snack!

Cupcake towers as a centerpiece,
Watch them collapse in a sugary fleece.
We burst into giggles; oh, what a treat,
As frosting decorates all we eat.

So raise your glass, let's cheer today,
For family, friends, in our own funny way.
Toasting to love, and silly delight,
Together we shine, oh what a sight!

A Gathering of Light

At Uncle Bob's with hats askew,
We passed the peas, but lost a shoe.
Grandma's pie, a daring feat,
We raced for seconds, oh what a treat!

The turkey danced on the floor so grand,
While kids played tag with a gravy brand.
A mountain of laughter filled the air,
As Aunt Sue laughed, 'I can't even share!'

Cousins fought over the couch's best spot,
While others debated if it was too hot.
With every bite, we squeezed more fun,
Who knew a meal could weigh a ton?

As day turned night, lights twinkled bright,
We shared our stories, a pure delight.
With smiles and quirks, we set our sights,
On pie-filled dreams and silly fights!

Songs of the Season

In the kitchen, pots and pans collide,
Mom sings off-key with turkey pride.
The dog howls along to the festive tune,
While the cat gives looks that surely festoon.

Cousins drum on the table with glee,
While Grandpa pretends he can still agree.
A dance-off breaks out with a crazy twist,
Even the broccoli gets caught in the mist!

Grandma's secret is a jiggle of joy,
As we all try to catch that last toy.
The air contains smells too wild to speak,
Even the broccoli's dancing, so geek!

Laughter erupts like popcorn in air,
With silly voices, we remedy despair.
Every note sung brings us so near,
That even the turkey begins to cheer!

Savoring the Silence

After the feast, we sunk in our seats,
Caught in a silence, trading our treats.
The only sound was a sly little snore,
From Cousin Tim, who could eat even more!

We gazed at the table, all lovingly spread,
With crumbs and leftovers, a feast of bread.
But Auntie Mary found the last roll,
And launched it at Jerry—what a goal!

A peaceful calm shared with sleepy eyes,
While dreams of dessert filled all the skies.
But whispers of mischief drifted around,
As we plotted to steal that last slice found.

In moments of silence, joy intertwined,
A harmony carried through hearts combined.
For these are the times we hold and embrace,
With giggles that dance and smiles on each face!

Threads of Tradition

With every year, we gather 'round,
To swap old tales and joys profound.
A peculiar hat is worn with pride,
While soup spills suddenly, who will decide?

Grandpa's stories grow taller each year,
No one believes him, but we all cheer.
With pie in hand and laughter high,
Uncle Joe cracks jokes that make us sigh!

Beneath the table, the dog claims a throne,
Whiskers twitching, he's never alone.
Sticky fingers grab the last of the spread,
While feasting on tales that dance in our head.

Each moment we share is woven quite tight,
With silly traditions that spark pure delight.
As we raise our glasses with joy and glee,
Cheers to this gathering, just you and me!

Savoring Shared Smiles

Gather round the table wide,
Turkey's done, but where's the pride?
Uncle Joe just spilled his drink,
He laughs so hard, we can't help think.

Grandma's pie is all the rage,
But who knew it would engage?
Cousins compete in dessert fights,
Sugar high turns into night bites.

We pass the rolls, then roll our eyes,
Auntie Sue tells the worst of lies.
Laughter echoes, fills the air,
With every bite, we shed our care.

Even the dog joins in the fun,
Sneaking scraps when we're not done.
Mom just sighs, then rolls her eyes,
But it's the joy—in laughter, we rise.

A Tapestry of Togetherness

At Family Fest the quirks collide,
We gather in where chaos resides.
Silly hats and goofy ties,
Worn by folks who love to prize.

Siblings tease with sly remarks,
As playful jabs find their marks.
Dancing like nobody cares,
In mismatched socks and messy hair.

The table groans with fervent glee,
A feast that's far from fancy-free.
Veggies overcooked—it's a crime,
Still, we dig in and pass the thyme.

Mom's sweet potato casserole,
Is a hit, or so we'll extol.
But each slice brings mentioned dread,
As Uncle Larry shares his spread.

Culinary Remembrance

In kitchens where aromas fly,
Grandpa's secret stew makes us sigh.
It bubbles up with tales galore,
Of wild adventures from yore-on-yore.

A sprinkle here, a pinch of that,
With every stir, we giggle and chat.
Remembering how mom burned the bread,
Yet somehow still, we ate it dead.

Pumpkin scraps on the floor we find,
As sister's baking was quite blind.
With icing fingers, we start to dance,
And risk the flour for a wild chance.

Recipes passed with laughter loud,
Mixing joy in every crowd.
The blending of flavors and hearts we feast,
A cherished moment, to say the least.

Autumn's Embrace

Leaves twirl down like golden curls,
In sweaters snug, the laughter swirls.
A feast of colors, sights so bright,
Yet Aunt Edna's jokes give us a fright.

Cider flows like wild delight,
The toasts go up to sky's new height.
Accidental spills bring comic glee,
Who knew dinner could come with a spree?

The dog is dressed like a big ole turkey,
And Cousin Tim thinks that's quite jerky.
Tickling feathers, we all collide,
In this warm hug, we try to hide.

With every chuckle, every cheer,
It's clear that love will always near.
So, raise a toast to our funny chase,
In autumn's warm and treasured embrace.

Milton Keynes UK
Ingram Content Group UK Ltd.
UKHW030750121124
451094UK00013B/825

9 789916 943335